IMAGES
of America

HOT SPRINGS
NATIONAL PARK

The Noble Fountain stands in front of the Superintendent's Office, which spans from the reservation years to the early national park days. Constructed in 1891, this building was initially designed to contain pumps for the thermal water system, but it was never used for that purpose. It was remodeled in 1898 to house the reservation superintendent's office when his workplace was moved out of his residence on Fountain Street. (Courtesy of Hot Springs National Park archives.)

ON THE COVER: Bathers came from all over the country to partake of the thermal waters flowing from the mountains in Hot Springs. These three men are enjoying a dip in the footbath spring called the "Corn Hole." Initially, conditions at the springs were rustic, but over time the facilities to "take the cure" became much more elaborate. (Courtesy of Hot Springs National Park archives.)

IMAGES
of America

HOT SPRINGS
NATIONAL PARK

Mary Bell Hill

ARCADIA
PUBLISHING

Published by Arcadia Publishing
Charleston, South Carolina

Printed in the United States of America

Library of Congress Control Number: 2014938043

For all general information, please contact Arcadia Publishing:
Telephone 843-853-2070
Fax 843-853-0044
E-mail sales@arcadiapublishing.com
For customer service and orders:
Toll-Free 1-888-313-2665

Visit us on the Internet at www.arcadiapublishing.com

To my parents, Joyce and Lavan Bell, who instilled in me a love of national parks, and to my husband, Tom Hill, who shares that love.

CONTENTS

ACKNOWLEDGMENTS

I would like to thank everyone who played a role in the creation of this book. Title manager Julia Simpson and publishing editor Lydia Rollins at Arcadia Publishing provided me with opportunity, inspiration, and encouragement throughout this project and helped keep me stay on track. A big thank-you goes to Hot Springs National Park superintendent Josie Fernandez for giving me access to the park's archival collection, and to chief of resource management and visitor services Mike Kusch, who took time from his busy schedule to review the manuscript. My thanks go to Liz Robbins and the staff at the Garland County Historical Society, who allowed me into their great collection of photographs and entertained me with dozens of stories about the city. I especially want to thank James O. Cary for being so kind to let me visit with him in his home in Dallas and to borrow a photograph of his father. It was an afternoon that I will not forget. Thank you also to my sports historian and great brother-in-law Mike Dugan for letting me use the photographs of his great-grandfather and providing me with information on the baseball players who made Hot Springs their second home. Thanks go to retired interpretive ranger Gail Payton Sears, who generously provided me with information on her great-grandfather and his career. My parents, Joyce and Lavan Bell, my sister Susan Bell Dugan, and my friend James Sanderson all get a huge thank-you for their proofreading, suggestions, and support that only made this project better. Most of all, I want to thank my wonderful husband, Tom Hill, the curator at the park, who answered endless questions with patience and lots of humor when I needed it.

Unless otherwise noted, photographs in this book are pulled from the Hot Springs National Park archives. Images from other sources are credited within their captions. All errors or omissions made in this manuscript are solely my responsibility.

INTRODUCTION

People have been coming to the area known today as Hot Springs National Park for thousands of years. Some came to quarry the smooth novaculite stone found in the surrounding hills, some to bathe in the soothing thermal waters pouring from Hot Springs Mountain, and, later, others to make a living off the hordes of road-weary travelers who trekked here. Many believed the hot springwater to be curative; some believed it to be mystical. All were looking for something unique in the narrow "Valley of the Vapors."

This area became part of the United States with the Louisiana Purchase in 1803. The region had already been explored by French trappers and mapped by the Spanish, and it was reasonably well known to many Americans. Yet, in 1804, Pres. Thomas Jefferson dispatched an exploratory party led by William Dunbar and George Hunter to survey the Ouachita River Basin and make scientific observations along the way. The expedition spent a month camped in the Hot Springs area, reporting back that people were already visiting and using the thermal springs seasonally. No permanent white residents were to be found in the area, but that would soon change.

The small and growing settlement around the "hot springs of the Washita" became part of the Territory of Arkansas when it was organized in July 1819. Realizing the potential medicinal value of the thermal waters to all citizens of the young nation, the territorial legislature first petitioned Congress in 1820 to reserve the area from the public domain. This appeal was finally heeded in 1832 with the creation of Hot Springs Reservation, one of the earliest land-conservation efforts in US history.

The first rudimentary facilities erected to accommodate bathers consisted of simple shanties of rough boards surrounding dugout pools at the sites of several springs. Early lodging facilities were very basic establishments. In fact, some indigent visitors camped out on the hillsides surrounding the valley. Later, as more and more people came to town and demanded better facilities, offerings began to improve. Small hotels sprang up, and better bathing establishments began to appear.

Federal regulation of bathing establishments and business practices tightened in 1877 when the first reservation superintendent was assigned to the area by the secretary of the interior. Shantytowns were eliminated, and rigorous rules and regulations were established and disseminated. Over the years, a progression of well-appointed wooden Victorian bathhouses replaced rough board shacks at the springs. Health-seekers and casual visitors alike arrived in ever-greater numbers, while businesses and improved lodging arose to serve this rising influx. Larger and more sanitary masonry bathhouses with marble and tile interiors eventually replaced their wooden predecessors, and bathhouse owners vied with each other to offer prospective patrons the best services and amenities. Beginning in 1910, government-appointed medical directors improved control of the sanitary and hygienic conditions in the bathing institutions, including the free bathhouse operated for indigents by the federal government. The once-sleepy little hamlet in the Arkansas wilderness found itself a national destination for sufferers with a variety of ills and physical complaints.

In 1916, the National Park Service was created as an agency of the Department of the Interior and given management authority over the growing system of national parks and monuments across the country, including Hot Springs Reservation. In 1921, with the support of park service director Stephen Mather, the 89-year-old Hot Springs Reservation was re-designated by Congress as Hot Springs National Park. Soon, the nation's bustling health resort was on its way to becoming the Great American Spa. Although many visitors made the trek to the waters for their ailments, others simply came for relaxing vacations with their families and friends, enjoying the natural wonders of the park.

The park and its bathing establishments reached their pinnacle shortly after World War II, when injured veterans drove the number of baths given in one year to well over one million in 1947. A decline in medicinal uses of the thermal water began, however, with the advent of improved medicines and treatments in the late 1940s. Hard times were soon to follow, as visitation declined and businesses failed. The grand old bathhouses began to close in the early 1960s and continued to dwindle through the early 1980s. Only one bathhouse, the Buckstaff, which opened in 1912, would survive through the lean years and never close its doors. The rest of the buildings along Bathhouse Row sat dilapidated and empty for several years, awaiting an uncertain future.

This downward trend began to abate in the late 1980s, when the National Park Service undertook a program of stabilization and rejuvenation, hinting at a bright future of adaptive reuse for the beautiful old buildings. Bathhouse Row was nominated to the National Register of Historic Places in 1974 and became a National Historic Landmark in 1987. The restored Fordyce reopened in 1989 as the park Visitor Center and Museum. The Quapaw was leased in 2007 for rehabilitation as an updated bathhouse and spa. The Lamar reopened in 2009 to house park office space; three years later, its lobby became the park store, the Bathhouse Row Emporium. The Superior reopened in 2013 as a craft brewery and distillery, and the Ozark Bathhouse is today seeing new life as the park's art gallery and cultural center. As of this writing, proposals are on the table for at least temporary use of all the remaining empty bathhouses.

Today, Hot Springs National Park encompasses only 5,549 acres and is the smallest of the 59 national parks. Yet, the park hosts more than 1.3 million visitors annually. Since 1904, more than 90 million visitors have come to Hot Springs National Park. The 47 hot springs continue to pour forth more than 750,000 gallons of clear, thermal water each day at an average temperature of 143 degrees, as they have done for millennia. Over the years, the park has proven its adaptability, surviving even the most arduous times and emerging as a bright jewel in the national park system.

One

"DISCOVERY" AND RESERVATION YEARS

Archeological evidence suggests that humans have inhabited the area that would become Hot Springs National Park for almost 10,000 years. Native Americans probably came to this place to quarry the unique Arkansas novaculite, fashioning the smooth, dense stone into fine tools and projectile points. Without a doubt, they also knew of the many cold-water springs in the region and the hot water flowing from the tufa embankment at the base of what would much later be called Hot Springs Mountain. Over the intervening years, historians, anthropologists, and others have speculated just how the Quapaw, Caddo, and other native inhabitants might have used, and felt about, the thermal water. A swirling mythology grew around the springs, one that still lingers today.

When Pres. Thomas Jefferson selected explorer William Dunbar and scientist George Hunter to investigate the Ouachita River Basin in the southern reaches of the Louisiana Purchase in 1804, the expedition elected to journey to the "hot springs of the Washita" because they were already known to residents of the fledgling United States. While examining the area, members of the expedition found the remnants of makeshift structures and other signs that Europeans had been frequenting the area and using the springs.

The first permanent white settlers came to the Hot Springs area within a few years of the Hunter-Dunbar Expedition. Log houses and rough boards went up around the thermal springs so that visitors could partake of the "healing waters" in some semblance of comfort. More and more travelers braved the wilderness to trek here in search of relief for their ailments. Soon, frame structures, simple "hotels," and other modest conveniences began to appear, replacing the primitive facilities. As fame of the thermal waters spread through the Eastern United States, a community began to take shape—one that not only used the thermal springs, but catered to a growing coterie of tourists. A pattern began to emerge for the future of this rudimentary spa in the middle of the southern wilds and, along with it, a desire to preserve it for everyone.

One of the first to record impressions of the springs was George Featherstonhaugh in *Excursion through the Slave States*. He arrived in 1834, discovering a small population renting lodgings to visitors. Unlike the pastoral scene depicted in this lithograph from his book, Featherstonhaugh describes accommodations as "four wretched-looking log cabins." Of the springs, he writes, "At least thirty-five in number falling into the brook, raised its temperature to that of a warm-bath."

Among the earliest permanent residents, John Percival and Hiram Whittington built crude wooden lodgings similar to this early cabin along Hot Springs Creek. Visitors seeking relief for their ailments would either share the limited cabin space with others or camp outdoors, all for the chance to bathe in the open springs nearby. Whittington also operated a store that provided basic necessities to bathers during their sojourn.

Even after the creation of Hot Springs Reservation in 1832, squatters continued to freely build campsites on federal land on Hot Springs Mountain. This is one of the encampments that sprang up near the springs, called "Ral City" (short for "neuralgia"), consisting of makeshift tents and cabins. Overcrowding and lack of sanitation in these camps aggravated the local population, businessmen, and bathhouse proprietors and eventually led to conflict.

The influx of indigent bathers to Ral City and other similar camps on the surrounding hillsides was a distinct nuisance to permanent residents of the valley. They considered the places to be disgraceful and the men who lived there to be deadbeats and ruffians. Many of the men who resided in these camps had been soldiers during the Civil War (1861–1865) and were seeking treatments for their wounds.

"Delmonico's Café" in Ral City was a soup kitchen established by New York City restaurateur Charles Delmonico. During a visit to the reservation for thermal baths, he noticed the plight of the indigent population on the mountainside and left funds with the superintendent upon his departure to sponsor a simple scullery to feed the hungry inhabitants.

This primitive wooden structure was built in an indigent encampment on the hillside above the hot springs nicknamed "City of Siloam." The first superintendent assigned to Hot Springs Reservation, retired Union general Benjamin Franklin Kelley, took office in 1877 and immediately set upon the eradication of these proliferating settlements of the poor on federal land.

The "Corn Hole" spring was believed to be advantageous for treating corns, bunions, and other disorders of the feet. It was used by both men and women for soaking, but the sexes were segregated to different times of day. A sign on the surrounding privacy screen warns bathers to leave the pool in a "sanitary condition."

In 1875, the Weir & George Iron & Magnesia Bathhouse, located on the site of today's Ozark Bathhouse, was accessed via a wooden footbridge over Hot Springs Creek. Even though bathhouse operators touted the various hot springs as good for different types of ailments, the water from each spring was actually no different from the others. Despite what bathers believed, soaking in one was much like soaking in any other.

Accessing some springs was occasionally a tricky affair for invalids seeking treatment. Wooden plank walkways and uneven rocky paths were difficult to negotiate on two legs, much less on crutches or in a wheelchair. However, believing certain springs to be good for specific ailments, patrons fought through all obstacles to reach the thermal water they thought would heal them.

The hot springwater is laden with minerals that form a type of porous stone called "tufa" when the water evaporates. This large tufa boulder sitting at the edge of Hot Springs Creek built up around Big Iron Spring, forming a natural basin. These visitors are drinking the thermal water directly from the spring, while pipes transport the water to nearby bathhouses.

Alum Spring was the only thermal spring located on the west side of Hot Springs Creek, situated about three feet above the stream. It averaged 133 degrees and discharged about four gallons per minute. Its white latticework enclosure stood just south of the Hale Bathhouse and Hotel. Visible below the springhouse are two visitors drinking the water. Above them on the bridge are three bathers returning from the bathhouse.

Without plumbing, transporting springwater to other areas of town could be difficult, but there were ways around it for imaginative entrepreneurs. Thermal water was not only used for bathing or treating ailments, but also to supply hotels and restaurants in the burgeoning city with drinking water. Magnesia Spring and the Government Free Bathhouse are visible in the background.

Rector's Bathhouse and the Arsenic Spring pavilion connected to the south end of the first Arlington Hotel. The wooden bridge in the foreground allowed visitors to cross Hot Springs Creek. Completed in 1881 by D.W. Hashal at a cost of about $13,400, this was proprietor Henry Massie Rector's second of four versions of his namesake bathhouse. Rector was the sixth governor of the state of Arkansas, serving from 1860 to 1862.

This tufa formation at the spring near the rear corner of the Big Iron Bathhouse was created as the thermal water flowed into Hot Springs Creek. The pipes visible in the upper right and lower left are transporting hot springwater to other bathhouses along the creek.

16

In September 1878, Superintendent Kelley ordered the removal of the crude structures covering the Ral Hole Spring and other "dugout" pools, citing the unsanitary conditions surrounding the improvised pools and the hordes of indigents using them. Local businessmen had been advocating the structures' elimination, claiming they were scenes of indecency and a genuine nuisance for the legitimate bathing establishments in the valley below. The closure of the Ral Hole prompted a large group of its outraged patrons to stage an "indignation meeting," during which inflammatory speeches decried Kelley's actions and threatened violence against local businesses and citizens. The crowd proceeded to build a new, larger structure over the spring in defiance of Kelley and the local US marshal. Kelley immediately requested the dispatch of federal troops from Little Rock to quell the threat of violence.

This wooden shelter was built by New Yorker Charles Leland over a pool he dug out around Mud Hole Spring to treat his gout. When his condition improved, he returned home, leaving the structure for the indigent. Thus, it became the first free bathhouse on Hot Springs Reservation, providing poor bathers with the same opportunity to use the thermal waters as the paying customers using the other bathhouses in town.

This white frame building over the Mud Hole replaced the earlier free bathhouse at the site and is officially the first government-operated free bathhouse on the reservation. Magnesia Springs, on the east bank of Hot Springs Creek, is located below the structure. At the center of the photograph, a wooden trough carrying thermal water traverses the hillside along the creek.

Fire has been a reoccurring problem in Hot Springs. A catastrophic blaze took place on March 5, 1878, destroying all structures within an area of the city on Reserve Street, Spring Street, and Central Avenue, from the Hot Springs Hotel to the Big Iron Bathhouse just south of the Arlington Hotel. Here, only a small shack has survived the inferno along this section of Hot Springs Creek.

Gov. Henry Rector moved the state records to his bathhouse, the Rector, when the capital in Little Rock was about to be taken by Federal troops in 1862. Although no battles were fought in Hot Springs, the town suffered from marauding bands of Union and Confederate sympathizers, who each in turn tried to burn down the entire town. The empty lots with chimneys testify to how successful they were.

This historical view of downtown Hot Springs in the 1870s was taken from a window of the Hot Springs Hotel looking north. The two-story building with the cupola in the center of the photograph is the American Hotel. All of the buildings along the right are early bathhouses, and the last structure with a flagpole on the roof is the first Arlington Hotel.

Located along the east side of Hot Springs Creek, Magnesia Springs was a popular drinking site for visitors. The spring was situated just below the Government Free Bathhouse, making it a convenient stop for indigent bathers. The sign above the spring not only announces its name, but also advertises safe deposits across the street.

An integral part of the thermal water treatment involved drinking the water from the springs. These two couples are sharing a cup from Spring No. 1 on Hot Springs Mountain. The 47 springs scattered across the slope of the mountain produce an average of more than 750,000 gallons of water per day.

This white frame building with columned porch was the first Maurice Bath House. It predated the later Victorian-style bathhouse of the same name. Samuel Fordyce and Charles Maurice built it when they were having difficulty obtaining an interest in one of the already existing bathhouses. Later, after they took over the Independent and began building their own bathhouses, this structure became the Monarch gambling saloon.

This antique stereograph of Barnes's Whetstone Quarry displays the large novaculite deposits that occur in the mountains around Hot Springs. Novaculite was mined by early native peoples because of its ability to be easily formed into a variety of tools and retain a sharp edge. Later, the rock was quarried by white residents to provide whetstones for sharpening knives and other metal tools.

Bathers relax in the interior of the Huffman and Hamilton Bathhouse. The building, originally known as the Hot Springs Bathhouse, was located adjacent to the Hot Springs Hotel. In 1871, it was acquired and renamed by John M. Huffman and his business partner Fred W. Hamilton. The Huffman and Hamilton Bathhouse operated until March 5, 1878, when a fire swept through multiple structures along Hot Springs Creek.

This early photograph of downtown Hot Springs shows how closely the buildings were constructed to the street. The second Hale Bathhouse (left) was constructed in 1880 on top of Hot Springs Creek to increase its access to a water supply. Although the street is dirt, the trolley car operates on tracks that run down the middle of the valley boulevard.

Bathhouse Row and the first Arlington Hotel (left) were very rustic in appearance in 1875. The buildings farther along the left side of the photograph are bathing establishments built over the available thermal springs and Hot Springs Creek. City businesses line the right side of the street.

Built by George M. French in 1877 for $18,400, the Big Iron Bathhouse had a wide wooden bridge to provide easy access to the facility located on the east side of Hot Springs Creek. Excavation for the building required the first blasting ever to be done around the thermal springs. The bathhouse was torn down in 1891 due to its dilapidated condition.

On January 1, 1912, the new Maurice Bathhouse was dedicated. To honor the day, a group gathered at the Maurice Spring for a commemorative photograph. William G. Maurice, the proprietor of the new bathhouse that bears his name, is at center in the first row, sporting a mustache and bowler hat. Bathhouse attendants, musicians, and guests surround the proud owner.

Arsenic Spring's ornate Victorian pavilion connected the new Rector Bathhouse with the first Arlington Hotel. Built as an extension of part of the Rector Bathhouse in 1881, the pavilion's positioning displeased reservation superintendent Benjamin Franklin Kelley. He felt that it blocked the circulation of air and light through the space. Despite this, the spring was a favorite photography spot for visitors to both establishments. These images show groups posing at the spring to commemorate their trip to the thermal waters. Eventually, the pavilion and the Rector would be incorporated into a new Arlington Bathhouse.

Christopher Columbus Cooper Jr. was hired in 1892 as the first Hot Springs Reservation policeman. His duties were to patrol on foot the park property adjacent to the hot springs and bathhouses, enforcing good order, preventing public nuisances, and arresting disorderly visitors. By 1910, Cooper had become the head male attendant and the assistant manager at the government-run free bathhouse.

Charles Henry Payton Jr. immigrated to the United States from England in 1854 and served in the Civil War with the 1st Arkansas Cavalry. A tailor by trade, he worked as the first night policeman at Hot Springs Reservation from 1896 to 1899. Continuing the tradition of family service to the park, his great-granddaughter Gail Payton Sears later worked at the park for 20 years.

After a fire that blazed through the city in 1878, the early 1880s heralded a change in the look of Bathhouse Row. Above, the Independent (left) boasts a wide bridge. Next door, the finishing touches are being put on the tower atop the Palace Bathhouse. The open access to Hot Springs Creek made it a convenient dumping site for all types of debris. Shown below, in the street view of the row looking north, are, from right to left, the Ozark, Magnesia, Palace, Independent, and Hale Bathhouses. The long wooden walkways span Hot Springs Creek and illustrate how perilously close the houses were built along the eastern bank. The telephone poles along the street were later removed and the wires rerouted to enhance the overall look of the reserve.

Built in the Victorian style in 1880, the third Hale Bathhouse was constructed using portions of the second as a base. Its decorative Mansard roof, named after the 17th-century architect Francois Mansart, was a popular building style from 1860 through the 1880s. Towels and sheets are hung to dry on the banister and on the clothesline strung between the posts on the right side of the building.

After patrons completed their baths for the day, they often wanted to find activities to occupy their spare time. They also wanted to see more sights than just the local bathing facilities. Enterprising locals began to offer tours on horseback or, as shown here, on mules to take bathers up the mountain trails surrounding the city. The reservation was evolving from simply a place for invalids to a popular vacation destination.

As the reputation of the city and the reservation bathhouses grew, cleanliness along Hot Springs Creek became an issue. In 1882, the government began planning construction of an arched enclosure for a portion of the creek, one that would improve sanitation, reduce flooding in the city, and provide a broad, attractive boulevard through town. Work began in 1883 on the archway, which ran for 3,500 feet from Whittington Avenue to near Malvern Avenue. At right, the arch has been completed in front of the Rammelsberg Bathhouse. Below is a photograph of construction of the junction of the arches spanning Hot Springs and Whittington Creeks at the intersection of Central and Park Avenues. The stone-arch construction project was later the subject of a Congressional hearing in Washington, DC. (At right, courtesy of the Garland County Historical Society.)

This early photograph of Central Avenue presents a wonderful view of the wooden structures of Bathhouse Row after 1888. Shown here are, from front to rear, the Superior, Old Hale, Independent, Palace, and Horseshoe Bathhouses. Along the street is the pavilion that covers the Alum Spring. Visible in the distance is the Army and Navy General Hospital and the tower of the Eastman Hotel.

The Government Free Bathhouse stood on this site, behind the Quapaw and Fordyce, from 1891 to 1923. These cooling towers and holding tanks had been used by it and other bathhouses to cool springwater, which was then mixed with the scalding-hot water coming straight from the ground. This made the temperature tolerable for bathers. Federal regulations, still in place today, prohibited mixing city water with springwater.

Named after Secretary of the Interior Lucius Quintus Cincinnatus Lamar, the first Lamar Bathhouse was built in 1888 in an unusual, asymmetrical Victorian style. Located on site No. 2 between the Rammelsberg and the Government Pump House at the south end of the row, the Lamar had 40 bathing tubs, for which it paid the government a water lease rate of $30 per tub per year.

Hot Springs Reservation superintendent William P. Parks, MD, assembled his staff in front of the Superintendent's Office for this c. 1914 photograph. Parks is seen in the center of the first row in the light-colored suit. His wife is seated beside him. Posing with Parks are some of the 30 members of the reservation workforce.

The red tile roof and white stucco walls of the Superintendent's Residence made a stunning appearance along Fountain Street. Designed by architect Phillip Van Patten, the house was home to superintendents from 1892 until 1913, after which the building became the residence of the assistant superintendent. In the ensuing years, the building began to deteriorate and was finally demolished in 1958.

The reservation greenhouse, built in 1902, nurtured plants such as banana trees and bedding plants for landscaping. The structure burned down in 1923, and the new greenhouse was moved farther east on Fountain Street, near the cold-water pavilion (far left). Trees, shrubs, and flowers were cultivated for plantings until the building was removed in 1933.

With the allocation of $549.89, the reservation built this maintenance shed in 1903. Using bricks available from the remodel of the Government Free Bathhouse, the 100-foot-by-20-foot structure was located on the slope behind the Superintendent's Residence on Fountain Street. It housed horses, mules, wagons, and other supplies needed to maintain the reservation grounds.

This six-room brick caretaker's cottage at the west end of Whittington Lake Park on Whittington Avenue was completed in 1910, replacing the old wooden gardener's house that had been built there in 1897. Its occupant was in charge of maintaining the 11-acre park located between West Mountain and Sugarloaf Mountain. The cottage was removed in 1975.

Originally named the Independent, this bathhouse's lease was purchased by Charles Maurice and Charles Converse in January 1892. They subsequently remodeled the old structure and reopened the business as the second Maurice Bathhouse in 1893. The moderately priced baths and the connections of son William Maurice with the entertainment industry made the bathhouse a success.

Often referred to as the White House, the first Ozark Bathhouse was located between the Magnesia and the Rammelsberg on the former location of the Weir and George Bathhouse, which burned down in the fire of 1878. The Ozark was initially owned by Samuel Fordyce, George D. Latta, and Charles Maurice, and the construction of this Victorian building in 1880 cost just over $16,000.

Built in 1890–1891, the third Government Free Bathhouse was a brick edifice on the site of the old Mud Hole, slightly behind the Horseshoe and Magnesia Bathhouses. Under the guidance of the reservation improvements officer, US Army lieutenant Robert R. Stevens, a paved entrance connected the bathhouse to the Magnolia Promenade. The bathhouse was remodeled in 1904 to provide additional dressing areas and steam heating.

Whittington Lake Reserve, designed in 1893, included two lakes with pavilions, five bridges, a tennis court, a music pavilion, and a carriage drive around the park. The lakes were initially praised for their beauty but were not very deep due to shallow bedrock in the area. When summer heat lowered the water in the ponds, they became stagnant. They were filled in with soil in 1905.

The new Rector Bathhouse, built in 1883, was the third facility constructed by Henry M. Rector. It was located just south of the second Arlington Hotel. Eventually, this building would be incorporated into the hotel as the Arlington Bathhouse, and Rector would move across Central Avenue to build his fourth bathhouse.

This street scene of Bathhouse Row shows the new lawns and trees that were planted after the arch was built over Hot Springs Creek. Shown here are, from left to right, the Horseshoe, Magnesia, Ozark, Rammelsberg, and Lamar Bathhouses. The 1891 Government Free Bathhouse is set back from the main row, located between the Horseshoe and the Magnesia. (Courtesy of Garland County Historical Society.)

Built over a spring, the Magnesia Bathhouse opened in 1888. At times considered an eyesore on the row and in need of renovation, the Magnesia did not close until December 1920. It was one of the last Victorian buildings to be replaced along Bathhouse Row. Today's Quapaw Bathhouse was erected over the combined site of this bathhouse and the Horseshoe. (Courtesy of Garland County Historical Society.)

The Cooper Brothers sightseeing tours brought visitors through the park in horse-drawn coaches to gain a better appreciation of the mountains. The company's livery stables were one of the many businesses destroyed by fire in the city in September 1913. Another of the Cooper brothers, Christopher, was the first reservation policeman.

Presidents were not the only prominent people who enjoyed the resort. Woodrow Wilson's vice president, Thomas R. Marshall, and his wife, Lois Irene Kimsey Marshall, made a visit in 1915. Shown here in the front row are, from left to right, Mayor McClendon, Mrs. David Crockett, Mrs. Davenport, Lois Marshall, Thomas R. Marshall (seated), Mrs. Parks, Col. Samuel Fordyce, Miss Fergusson, Mrs. McClendon, and Mrs. Hobson.

Originally called Hale Spring, the Maurice Spring is located in an elevated plaza built into the tufa bluff along the base of Hot Springs Mountain. In 1896, Superintendent Little replaced its original walls with novaculite coped with white limestone. On the far right is Civil War veteran Patrick Dugan, who later became forester for the reservation. (Photograph by M.L. Fuller, courtesy of the US Geological Survey.)

To encourage visitors to enjoy all aspects of their time at the thermal waters, trails were developed on the mountainsides. This trail along the west slope of Hot Springs Mountain had markers informing hikers of the distance they had traveled. Called the Oertel Fitness Trail, it had four levels of difficulty for each color of trail, labeled yellow, green, blue, and red.

A crowd gathers at the opening of the second Lamar Bathhouse in April 1923. Construction started in 1922 to replace the old wooden building with a sanitary masonry, stone, and brick structure. Boasting a gymnasium used by both men and women and a large lobby and sun porch, this new bathhouse would operate for 62 years.

Supt. William P. Parks (center) and a group of rangers pose in front of the old headquarters building. Parks, the last superintendent of Hot Springs Reservation, helped usher in the new designation of Hot Springs National Park as its first superintendent. Instrumental in changing the look of the landscape, Dr. Parks introduced the Oertel Trail System to Hot Springs Mountain in order to promote health and enjoyment for visitors.

Hot Springs advertised itself as a place that was monitored and safe for everyone to visit. This image from a brochure shows the Stevens Balustrade with baseball players, women, children, and military personnel being watched over by a park ranger on horseback. Health and pleasure were to be safely had by bathing at the government's thermal waters.

Two

BECOMING AMERICA'S SPA

Largely through the promotion and zeal of Stephen T. Mather, the first director of the National Park Service, Congress redesignated Hot Springs Reservation as Hot Springs National Park on March 4, 1921. The popular park was by this time a world-famous destination for not only those seeking cures for various ailments, but for people looking for simple relaxation and enjoyment in a resort environment. A trip to the grand establishments along Bathhouse Row was considered essential for restoring good health and vitality to life. The tremendous influx of patrons, however, not only changed the services that were offered, but altered the face of the park itself.

The progression of government-owned free bathhouses would culminate with the opening of a state-of-the-art facility in 1922. (This would later become known as the Libbey Physical Medicine Center.) In the 1930s, the park service would perfect an efficient thermal water-collection system, featuring large underground-holding reservoirs and an elaborate pumping network, allowing plenty of thermal springwater to be available to all the bathhouses calling for it. A new facility to house the park maintenance division would be erected on Whittington Avenue in the mid-1930s. Work would begin on the Grand Promenade on the hillside behind Bathhouse Row, from Reserve Street in the south to Fountain Street in the north. A new park Administration Building would replace the old Superintendent's Office at the corner of Reserve Street and Central Avenue in 1935. And, the stately Victorian Superintendent's Residence on Fountain Street would be torn down to complete the wooded foreground at the north end of the Grand Promenade. But, the introduction of new medicines and therapeutic practices occasioned by World War II would portend great changes for the bathing industry in Hot Springs.

This panoramic view of Hot Springs from a tourist brochure, "Hot Springs in a Nutshell," shows the expansion of the valley. Taken from the top floor of the Eastman Hotel, the photograph shows the Imperial Bathhouse with the Superintendent's Office at the south end of the reservation. Visible behind them are the Lamar and Rammelsberg Bathhouses. The second Arlington Hotel is at the far end of Bathhouse Row.

The first version of the Maurice Bathhouse was a Victorian wooden building with large windows in the lobby. The long walkway and wide expanse of sidewalk were installed after Hot Springs Creek was covered with an arch. Three rows of trees were established between the buildings and the street, the last being the magnolias.

The sun porch at the first Lamar Bathhouse was narrow and often crowded with customers waiting for their time in the baths. Although it was supposed to be a place to relax, these patrons look anything but in the congested space. Note that the women are at the far end, away from the men with cigars.

Samuel Fordyce's Palace Bathhouse, built in 1888, was a step above many of the other businesses. Situated on the site of the New Central Bathhouse, the Palace was stocked with porcelain tubs for the bathers' comfort. Operating until the end of 1913, the building was torn down and replaced with the new Fordyce Bathhouse.

Starting with the second Arlington Hotel (left foreground), changes are apparent in the park in 1911. The absence of the Rector Bathhouse has left a green space next to the Superior, and cooling tanks are visible behind this bathhouse. Next is the Old Hale, with its name printed on its domed roof, followed by the second Maurice, which is under construction. Horses and trolleys run on Central Avenue.

In 1892, the old Rector on the east side of Central Avenue was demolished to make way for the new Arlington Bathhouse. A new Rector (right) opened on the west side of the street in 1895. The bathhouse was outfitted with men's and women's parlors and had a connecting bridge to the Waukesha Hotel next door.

A Grecian pavilion built in 1897 sits atop Alum Spring in front of Hale Bathhouse. The pavilion would later be renamed the Major Harry M. Hallock Fountain after the reservation medical director who served from 1909 to 1913. The spring was covered in 1921 as part of renovations in the park. This fourth version of the Hale was completed in 1892 on the same site of the previous Victorian version.

As visitors flocked to the resort, the park made changes to provide access to the thermal drinking water for everyone. Noble Fountain was installed at the south end of Bathhouse Row at the corner of Central Avenue and Reserve Street. Its bronze eagles were designed by the famous sculptor Edward Kemeys. This convenient location quickly became a gathering spot for locals and out-of-town guests.

Assistant Secretary of the Interior Stephen T. Mather poses on horseback in Happy Hollow while visiting Hot Springs in November 1915. Mather was an enthusiastic supporter of Hot Springs even before he was named the first director of the National Park Service in May 1917. He showed a keen interest in the park's affairs, even remarking that Hot Springs had not been "thoroughly appreciated" in the past. The fact that Hot Springs Reservation was renamed Hot Springs National Park by Congress in 1921 is directly attributable to Mather's recognition of its importance and his political influence in Washington, DC. Unknown to many, Mather suffered for most of his adult life from bipolar disorder, enduring incapacitating stress-induced mood swings that periodically required his extended confinement in a sanitarium or hospital. Afterward, he would quietly retreat to the majestic scenery of one of his beloved national parks to recuperate, surrounded by nature. On at least one of these occasions Mather came to Hot Springs to recover in the familiar confines of the Fordyce Bathhouse, where he bathed and relaxed with massages.

The Rammelsberg (left) and the Lamar together anchor the south end of Bathhouse Row. A sign on the Rammelsberg advertises 21 baths for the rate of $3. The roof of the Imperial Bathhouse is barely visible behind the Lamar. On the hill above is the Army and Navy General Hospital and, on the far right, the expansive Eastman Hotel.

Over time, Bathhouse Row was being slowly molded into a more park-like setting. The magnolia trees along the street were planted in 1893 and 1894. The buildings lining the street are, from near to far, the Horseshoe, with its distinctive white circular window trim, the Palace, and the Maurice. At the far left end of the street is the second Arlington Hotel.

With its imposing facade, the Ozark Bathhouse towers over its smaller neighbor, the Magnesia. Since its original construction in 1880, the Ozark had been renovated to install tile floors and fashionable porcelain tubs. The top floor and rounded roof of the Government Free Bathhouse can be seen behind the Magnesia.

All of the members of this family ride together in a four-in-hand coach approaching Hot Springs Mountain. The sightseeing tours run by the Cooper Brothers Livery Stables took tourists up and down the gravel Pleasure Drive and Carriage Road, enabling them to enjoy the natural surroundings of the beautiful resort while in town to seek treatment for their health.

The Dugan family poses for a photograph in front of their residence, the Caretaker's Cottage in Whittington Park. Patrick Dugan, a Civil War veteran, came to town for treatment of war wounds and later became the reservation forester. Posing here are, from left to right, John, Dan, Mary, Patrick, Billy, Maggie, Henry, and Jimmy. The cottage is in the background on the left, partially obscured by trees. (Courtesy of Jerome Michael Dugan.)

Initially called the Whittington Avenue Lake Reserve, this tranquil lake on the 11-acre Whittington Park site is seen here. A trolley passes on the left. Limestone posts were placed at the park's entrance, and an iron fence enclosed the property. The fence was washed away during a flood in 1923.

This photograph of the finely landscaped circular island between the lakes at Whittington Park shows one of the five bridges that were constructed across the lagoons. Water flow was a constant problem, and the lakes were eventually replaced with open expanses of lawn. Stone retaining walls enclosed the creek and helped alleviate erosion effects. (Courtesy of Garland County Historical Society.)

This photograph, taken after 1921, displays the name Hot Springs National Park on the left column of the Superintendent's Office, located at the corner of Central Avenue and Reserve Street. The original building was constructed of brick and stone and painted white. Supt. William Little moved his office from the residence on Fountain Street to this building after it was remodeled in 1898.

A road to the top of West Mountain had first been proposed by Lt. Robert Stevens in 1894, but it was not completed until 1901. The road was originally restricted to horse-drawn vehicles, but in 1916 the Department of Interior made it the only roadway in the park cleared for automobiles. On February 14, 1920, Gen. John J. Pershing officiated at a ceremony that opened all park roads for automobile travel.

The towers of the Arlington Hotel stand out in a south-facing photograph of Hot Springs. This second version of the hotel was erected on park property in 1893. The Superior, Hale, and the white square structure of the Maurice Bathhouse are visible beyond the hotel. (Photograph by H.D. Miser, courtesy of the US Geological Survey.)

At the summit of Hot Springs Mountain, an 80-foot wooden tower was built in 1877 to provide panoramic vistas to anyone who made the ascent. After it was struck by lightning and burned down, a steel tower was put in its place by the Texas Steel Bridge Company in 1906. Equipped with stairs and an elevator, the 185-foot tower was a huge success. Access to the tower cost 25¢ for each adult.

This aerial photograph of Hot Springs Mountain, taken from an overlook on West Mountain Drive, shows the extent of the hiking trails and roads over the hillside. In the lower-right corner, the dome of the Quapaw is visible above the trees; the two square buildings with three windows are the cooling towers for the bathhouses.

With the Palace Bathhouse closing in 1914, the site was readied for the next generation of bathhouse. An initial job to be completed was the excavation and construction of new basement walls and a water reservoir (above). The side of the wooden Horseshoe Bathhouse is visible in the upper left. Built at a cost of $200,000, the new structure, called the Fordyce Bathhouse, would need a dependable flow of thermal water. Drilling a new well on the south side of the Fordyce (at right) are John Fordyce, in the center with clipboard in hand, and Jack Manier, manager of the new bathhouse, to the right of Fordyce.

Samuel Fordyce poses in front of his new bathhouse. A businessman from St. Louis, Fordyce initially came to town seeking relief for his health problems in 1873. He became enamored of the healing abilities of the waters. He moved his family to the city in 1876. Fordyce's investments not only included his magnificent bathhouse, but the city opera house, municipal utility systems, hotels, a country club, and the city streetcar system.

The Fordyce was designed to be one of the most opulent buildings on Bathhouse Row, and its construction drew wide interest from not only future patrons, but other bathhouse owners as well. Building on the site of the former Palace Bathhouse, Samuel Fordyce raised the quality of the bathing experience, with stained-glass windows, imported marble bathing enclosures, and innovative Zander physical-therapy equipment.

A music room on the third floor of the Fordyce Bathhouse gave ladies and gentlemen a place to relax, visit with friends, or write letters before or after their baths. From the stained-glass ceiling to the elegantly tiled floor, patrons knew they were in the best facility. A screen at the end of the room closes off the ladies' private parlor; men had their own at the opposite end.

Once inside a bathhouse, patrons would be guided by attendants through their thermal bathing regimen. The ladies bath hall in the Quapaw was filled with diffused illumination from the overhead skylights, and the individual stalls were tiled to provide a hygienic environment. The relaxing atmosphere left visitors feeling rejuvenated and renewed.

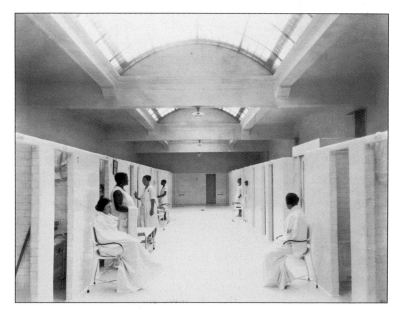

The 1932 National Park Service Superintendents' Conference was held at Hot Springs National Park, with much of the discussion centered on master planning for parks. In this official conference photograph, Supt. Thomas J. Allen is fourth from the right in the front row, and Director Horace is fifth from the right in the front row. This photograph was taken in front of the Superintendent's Office building at the south end of Bathhouse Row.

Named after Army lieutenant Robert R. Stevens, the Hot Springs Reservation improvements officer, Stevens Balustrade, was designed to present a formal entrance to the park, with an enclosed shell fountain and stone steps leading to a hillside bandstand. Lit at night with streetlamps, the bandstand provided a place for musicians to serenade strolling tourists.

Once West Mountain Drive was carved out of the mountainside, it became a task to keep the packed dirt road usable. Heavy rains would cause soil to slide or slump onto the roadway. Here, park maintenance workers install log cribbing to help retain a slope. The road would be paved by 1937.

In March 1933, the Civilian Conservation Corps (CCC) was formed as one of President Roosevelt's New Deal proposals to combat the economic effects of the Great Depression. The plan was to engage a quarter of a million unemployed men in public works and conservation projects across the country, primarily within national parks and forests. That May, a CCC camp was established near Hot Springs National Park to assist for six months.

The men's bath hall in the Fordyce was elegantly furnished with a stained-glass ceiling, marble bath stalls, and a large fountain depicting explorer Hernando de Soto receiving a cup of thermal water from a young Native American woman. The five patrons are being cared for by two African American bath attendants.

As part of their therapy, patients were taken to the basement of the Maurice to the thermal pool. There, they would be helped by attendants to utilize exercise equipment, seen here along the left side of the pool. Patrons with limited mobility were floated on cots while their limbs were massaged by the therapists.

When the Sells Floto Circus visited Little Rock, the manager of the Fordyce, Joseph Manier, found a way to advertise the bathhouse at the state capital. Manier paid $20 to place a large hand-painted sign on the elephant so that everyone who attended the circus would also think about traveling to Hot Springs for a bath.

Built in 1896, the Marine Bandstand Pavilion above the Stevens Balustrade was a venue for concerts and musical interludes for the next 30 years. A pathway at the back of the bandstand allowed patients from the Army and Navy General Hospital, located just behind the bathhouses, to access the area by the carriage road.

As its notoriety grew, Hot Springs National Park became a welcome stop for many athletes. Famed boxer Jack Dempsey (second from left) strolls the park trails with two unidentified men and his movie-star wife, Estelle Taylor. Dempsey was there to meet with boxing promoter Tex Rickard, who was in town taking the baths. It was during this visit that the bout with Gene Tunney was planned. (Courtesy of Garland County Historical Society.)

Hattie Caraway of Arkansas was the first woman elected to the US Senate, the first woman to preside over the Senate, and the first woman to chair a Senate committee. Serving from 1932 to 1945, she supported Pres. Franklin D. Roosevelt's economic recovery legislation during the Depression. She and the rest of the Arkansas congressional delegation accompanied Roosevelt when he visited Hot Springs National Park in 1936.

Erosion of the precipitous slopes along West Mountain was often a problem during heavy rains. Stone retaining walls were installed on the south-facing slope in 1914 in an effort to put an end to these slumping issues. Above, unidentified park maintenance workers stand proudly with their completed stair-step retaining walls. The photograph below is of the same location along the road in 1925. The stone walls are still standing and have become part of the overall terrain of the hillside. Automobiles, horses, and pedestrians often shared the road to partake of the natural wonders of the park.

On May 14, 1923, a catastrophic flood left Central Avenue with nine feet of water rushing through it. During the event, four feet of water rose on Bathhouse Row, but the businesses were still able to open to patrons. Once the floodwaters receded, the people of Hot Springs began the arduous task of cleaning up the debris on Central Avenue. The photograph above shows the street pavement in front of the Lamar Bathhouse broken into large slabs. The image below depicts two cars that were washed away during the flood and wedged into the trees in front of the Fordyce Bathhouse. In the foreground, the old brick street and trolley tracks are visible since the covering pavement was washed away during the deluge. This would not be the last flood to threaten the city. (Author's collection.)

As the Superintendent's Office began to show its age, plans were discussed to remove the building and replace it with a new facility. New sidewalk plantings and the installation of the Noble Fountain had made the corner a natural gathering place for visitors. A sign for the new Imperial Bathhouse is visible above the roof of the Superintendent's Office.

In 1936, construction began on Public Works Administration (PWA) Project No. 534, and the new park Administration Building began to take shape. This building would house not only administration functions, but also contain a visitor center and museum. These new amenities for guests would remain in this building until the renovation of the Fordyce Bathhouse into the park Visitor Center and Museum in 1989.

Located two miles northeast of Bathhouse Row, the park's only campground has long been a popular destination for visitors wishing to commune with nature. The property was donated to the park by John Fordyce through the Hot Springs Chamber of Commerce in late 1924. It had originally been a camping area located on the Fordyce estate. A new entrance was added with stone pillars to attract visitors to the campsite.

An early photograph of the changing stations at Gulpha Gorge shows the rustic buildings for both boys and girls. During the intense summers, the swimming pool was the best place to cool off. The area was formally named Gulpha Gorge Campground in 1939 by Supt. Preston Patraw so that the campground would have a "distinctive" name like other places within the National Park System.

A swimming pool already existed at the automobile tourist camp in Gulpha Gorge when it was donated to the park in 1924, but park workers immediately deepened and cleaned it. In 1933, the entire campground was upgraded by CCC workers, who excavated the swimming pool to make it larger. It was a popular spot in the heat of summer, attracting locals and park visitors alike.

As Americans began to take more leisure time after World War II, the campground and picnic area in Gulpha Gorge Campground became a destination for visitors from out of town. New campsites were laid out to accommodate the growing trend of families heading to the National Parks with a camping trailer for recreation.

First authorized by Congress in 1892, plans for the Whittington Avenue Lake Reserve were not finalized until early 1896. Work on the site began later that year, and the project was completed in 1897. The finished park originally featured two boating lakes with observation pavilions, five bridges over Whittington Creek, a music pavilion, carriage drives, and this tennis court with two spectator pavilions.

This photograph from the spring of 1934 shows construction progress on the new park maintenance and utility complex on Whittington Avenue. The tennis court and spectator pavilions at the west end of Whittington Park are visible in the background. The new maintenance complex, built with WPA funding, was completed in 1936.

Many popular entertainers visited the Hot Springs area for a chance to relax, including radio singer Kate Smith. Unfortunately, during Smith's stay at the Mountain Valley Hotel in 1934, the facility caught fire and burned to the ground. Although uninjured, she lost everything, including her luggage. The undaunted Smith was able to supplement her remaining wardrobe with a bath towel from the park.

International personalities often made their way to Hot Springs. Opera soprano Lily Pons made a trip to the park and visited the display springs. The French-born singer was the principal soprano at the Metropolitan Opera in New York from 1931 until 1960, and she starred in three films, including *That Girl from Paris*, which was mentioned by Harry Truman in a letter home during his sojourn in the park in 1937.

When Lt. Robert Stevens was selected by Secretary of the Interior John Noble in 1892 as the reservation improvements officer for Hot Springs, he immediately contacted the firm of noted landscape architect Frederick Law Olmsted. After a frustrating and brief collaboration, during which few actual plans were created, that relationship was terminated. Stevens selected other designers. One of the few Olmsted design elements to be used was the decorative stone columns that flank the formal entrance. Completed in 1893, the columns feature large bronze eagles by sculptor Edward Kemeys. The photograph above shows the formal entrance columns, Stevens Balustrade, and the bandstand between the Maurice and Fordyce prior to the paving of the carriageway between the buildings in the 1920s. Below, park maintenance personnel sandblast the columns to clean them in the 1930s.

As part of their bathing amenities, many bathhouses offered patrons the services of professional masseurs and therapists. In the early 1920s, the Men's Massage Room at the Quapaw Bathhouse was equipped with state-of-the-art electro-mechanical therapy machines, like that in the cabinet on wall to the left, and the small electrical generator on the table.

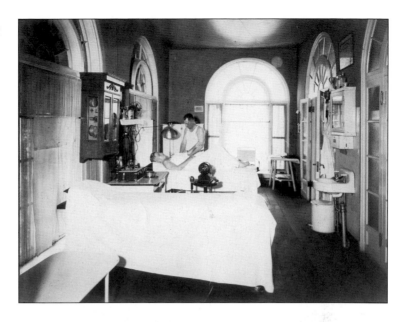

The Magnesia Spring in Happy Hollow on Fountain Street became part of Hot Springs National Park in November 1959, when Supt. Raymond Gregg exchanged parkland behind the Arlington Hotel to the Arlington Hotel Company for the nonfederal inholding surrounding Happy Hollow Spring. A new jug fountain plaza to replace the old facility was immediately begun, and the refurbished Happy Hollow Spring was officially opened on April 1, 1960.

Hot Springs National Park ranger James Alexander Cary was the first National Park Service ranger to be murdered in the line of duty. Ranger Cary had been with the park service since 1923 and previously served in the US Navy aboard the USS *Orient* in World War I. Cary was to testify in a court case against bootleggers operating in the park, but before the trial was held, he was ambushed and shot while patrolling West Mountain on March 12, 1927. When he failed to return home in the evening, he was reported missing, and a search began on West Mountain at the site of Cary's empty patrol car. His body was not located until the next day. It was found on the mountainside by several members of his family. A lengthy investigation involving an undercover FBI agent culminated in the arrest of five local men. Although these suspects went on trial for Cary's murder, no one was ever convicted of the crime. (Courtesy of James O. Cary.)

For years, Iron Spring in Gulpha Gorge Campground had been popular with visitors for its cool, refreshing water. It had no connection with the thermal springs on the opposite side of Hot Springs Mountain. In 1957, it tested positive for contamination and was closed. The water was diverted into Gulpha Creek.

Long a proponent of thermal hydrotherapy, Pres. Franklin Roosevelt visited the park in 1936 during the Arkansas centennial celebration. Riding in the jump seat in front of the president is former park superintendent Thomas Allen, recalled from his new post at Rocky Mountain National Park specifically for the president's visit. After an inspection of the bathhouses, Allen accompanied the presidential party on a drive over the new West Mountain road.

Completed in 1893, the Imperial anchored the south end of the reservation on the former site of the Huffman-Hamilton Bathhouse. The imposing brick structure was the most elaborate bathhouse until the construction of the new Fordyce in 1915. Offering individual dressing rooms and a gymnasium, it was a step above the wooden bathhouses. The Imperial was torn down in 1937 to make way for the southern entrance of the Grand Promenade.

Grading and excavating for construction of the Grand Promenade began in 1933. Here, a worker breaks up a large tufa dome with a jackhammer. This wide walking path was designed to traverse the hillside just behind Bathhouse Row, from Reserve Street to Fountain Street. It would not be completed as originally planned until 1958. It was made a National Recreational Trail on April 14, 1982.

With the help of public works funds, Gulpha Gorge Campground was updated to handle the large crowds with a new sewage system, a changing building, and renovations to the swimming area. By the 1940s, the swimming pool had become contaminated and was closed by the Public Health Service. Park maintenance workers removed the dam, allowing the water to drain into the creek, and restored the landscape to a more natural setting.

A severe flash flood on July 16, 1963, caused considerable damage downtown and to campsites and picnic areas in Gulpha Gorge Campground. The bridge across Gulpha Creek to Iron Spring was also damaged by a logjam of uprooted trees. Bulldozers were brought in to make repairs and clear rocks and debris from the creek bed. Here, they are clearing the area near Iron Spring.

Downtown Hot Springs is seen here in the mid-1920s. The south-facing photograph, showing Central Avenue, was taken from atop the third Arlington Hotel. Arlington Lawn, in the foreground, was the location of the second Arlington Hotel, which burned down in April 1923. The Superior Bathhouse is visible at the far end of the lawn.

Arlington Lawn and the new Arlington Hotel are seen here in the mid-1920s. The photograph looks north from the Superior Bathhouse. The Hoke Smith Fountain is visible to the left at the intersection of the sidewalks. This columnar drinking fountain of white sandstone and marble, with four discharge pipes at its base, was completed in 1897. It was lighted at night to make thermal water continuously accessible to the public.

The second Arlington Hotel opened on March 25, 1893. The four-story, red-brick structure built in Spanish Renaissance architectural style replaced the earlier, wooden, three-story version and was called the New Arlington. It featured 300 guest rooms and imposing twin towers flanking its Central Avenue facade. The hotel burned down on April 5, 1923. (Author's collection.)

Miraculously, despite having around 500 guests registered at the time it burned down, only one person, a 42-year-old Hot Springs fireman named George D. Ford, was killed in the Arlington Hotel fire. He and two other firefighters were caught in the collapse of a brick wall, but the other two men survived the accident. (Author's collection.)

This 1924 photograph of construction of the third Arlington Hotel was taken looking north from the roof of the Superior Bathhouse. The "Texas Star" flower garden is visible in the foreground. The site of the previous two Arlington Hotels is being used as a staging area for construction materials. When the 560-room hotel opened, the site of its predecessors was turned into what is today called Arlington Lawn.

Looking south from the construction site of the third Arlington Hotel in 1924, the Superior Bathhouse is visible in the distance. Building materials as well as brick and debris from the second Arlington Hotel cover "Arlington Lawn" and make Fountain Street almost impassable. The tufa-covered lower slopes of Hot Springs Mountain are also clearly visible to the left of the Superior.

These professional baseball players are hiking on mountains in the park as part of their preparation for the coming season. Hot Springs was the first home of spring training for many major-league teams. Pitcher Walter Johnson of the Washington Senators, fourth from the left, was one of many big-league players who chose to return to Hot Springs yearly on their own for preseason training.

Some big-league baseball teams started coming to Hot Springs as early as 1886 to use the thermal waters and local terrain to train for the upcoming season. Players visited various bathhouses for soaking and massage after practicing at local ball fields. Here, George Livingston Earnshaw, pitcher for the Chicago White Sox, enjoys a steam cabinet in Hot Springs National Park in the 1930s.

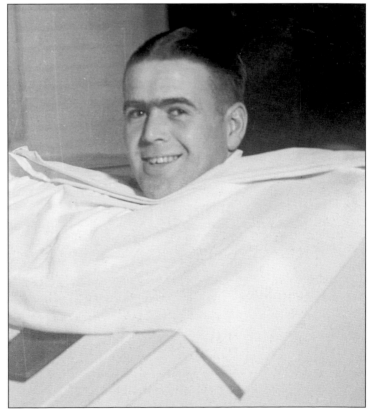

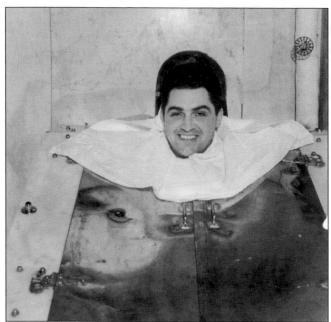

Washington Senators pitcher Earl Whitehill, enjoying his time in the steam cabinet, was one of many players who regularly made the trip to the thermal waters to "boil-out" and prepare for the upcoming baseball season. Not only would the players partake of the baths, they often hiked on the mountain trails to help get in shape.

Gordon Stanley "Mickey" Cochrane, player-manager of the Detroit Tigers from 1934 to 1938, has a thermal bath in the Maurice Bathhouse. By the 1940s, teams stopped coming to Hot Springs in favor of other locales, but the city had helped establish the spring-training tradition in major-league baseball.

In late April 1939, while conducting field maneuvers en route to artillery training exercises at Fort Sill, Oklahoma, the 1st Field Artillery Observation Battalion from Fort Bragg, North Carolina, camped briefly at the park's Gulpha Gorge Campground. Scores of military-issue, two-man pup tents dotted the entire campsite during their stay.

Troops of the Army's 1st Field Artillery Observation Battalion line up beside their transport vehicles while encamped at Gulpha Gorge Campground on April 26, 1939. Military personnel would be frequent visitors to the park in the coming war years due to the proximity of the Army and Navy General Hospital on the hillside above Bathhouse Row.

This photograph from early 1921 was taken in the pit left behind by the demolition of the Magnesia Bathhouse. The open ground between here and the Fordyce in the background had been vacated by the demolition of the Horseshoe Bathhouse in 1917. These two lots were to be the location of the new Platt Bathhouse, which was renamed the Quapaw Bathhouse before it was completed in 1922.

The new Government Free Bathhouse was dedicated on November 14, 1921, and it opened for business the following March. It would be the only bathhouse on government property not on Bathhouse Row. This view shows the fixtures and amenities in one bathing area, including a private toilet and private shower stall.

Hot Springs National Park has always been more than just Bathhouse Row in the historic district downtown. It also encompasses 5,549 acres of forested hills and mountains. To encourage guests to exercise during their visits, hiking trails were carved along the five surrounding mountains. Rangers conducted nature hikes along these trails, such as this trip to Goat Rock in the 1940s with Ranger Irving Townsend and two unidentified visitors.

The US Navy Band from the Army and Navy General Hospital often gave public concerts from atop the Stevens Balustrade after the removal of the bandstand pavilion above. The remnant balcony of the old Navy bandstand is visible to the upper left, and the hospital buildings are evident through the trees in the background.

A quartet of women bedecked in brightly striped bathrobes and holding Hot Springs National Park towels prepares to record a promotional radio spot. The women are, from left to right, Wilda Martin (pianist), Rena Stearns, Alice Freeman, and Marguerite Runyan. They were singing about the "three *Rs*: Rest, Recreate, and Recuperate."

Bathhouse Row was often touted in promotional literature as the "Showplace of Hot Springs National Park." This scenic view is of the wide Magnolia Promenade looking north from the Lamar Bathhouse toward the Ozark Bathhouse in the distance. A row of shade trees lines the sidewalk along its eastern side.

The dome of the Quapaw Bathhouse shines in the afternoon sun in this view looking north along Bathhouse Row. The Arlington Hotel is visible in the distance. By this time, the row of shade trees along the east side of the sidewalk have been removed, with only the magnolias along Central Avenue and a few of the American holly trees on the lawns remaining.

This photograph of Bathhouse Row, looking north along Central Avenue, dates from the 1950s. The old Army and Navy General Hospital is on the hillside to the right, and the Arlington Hotel and Medical Arts Building are seen in the distance on the left. The south entrance to the Grand Promenade, at this time still a simple wooden stairway, is visible at the right edge.

The park's campground and picnic area along Gulpha Creek have always been utilized heavily by the public. This scene from the late 1950s shows the range of users, from tents to trailers. As automobile travel increased after World War II, the campground continually evolved to accommodate a more mobile society.

When the Prospect Avenue entrance to West Mountain Drive was completed in November 1941, motorists could access the mountain from farther west along Prospect Avenue than in previous years using the Hawthorn Street entrance. Although it has changed in appearance over the years, this is still the southern entrance to West Mountain.

Promotional materials and advertisements for Hot Springs National Park have for years featured Uncle Sam with the slogan "Uncle Sam Bathes the World at Hot Springs, Arkansas." The bathing industry frequently capitalized on the fact that the federal government was regulating and controlling the thermal water and its use, making it safe for patrons.

UNCLE SAM BATHES THE WORLD AT HOT SPRINGS, ARKANSAS

Quapaw Bathhouse attendant Voncile Payton takes care of a bather in the 1950s. Bathhouses utilized bathing attendants as early as 1875 to provide patrons with personal assistance and individual therapy. By 1910, the federal government issued regulations limiting the amount of work an attendant could be assigned. The majority of bathing attendants were African Americans, who were not allowed to use most of the bathhouses along Bathhouse Row until after desegregation.

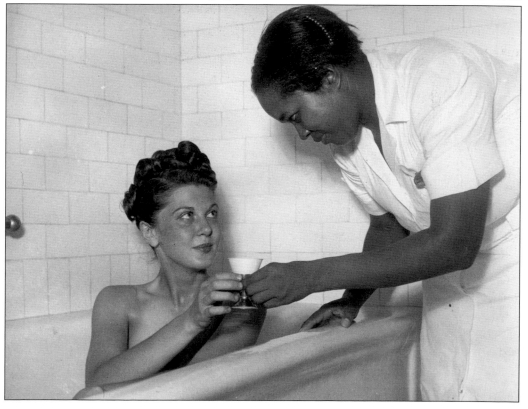

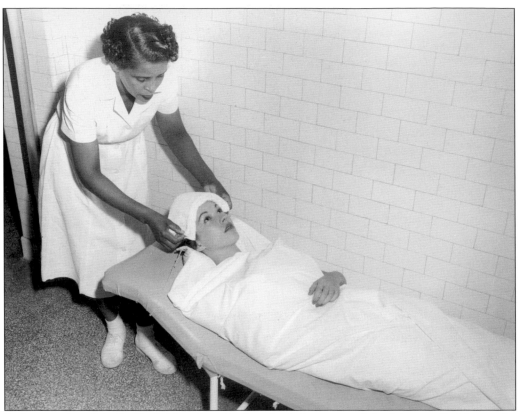

Bath attendant Iola Bedford (above) worked in the ladies areas of the Maurice Bathhouse for many years. Here, she is placing a cool towel on the forehead of a female patron resting in the pack room. Bath attendants monitored and timed baths and other activities to ensure the safety of patrons. They also served cooled thermal drinking water as part of the regimen. Attendant Ernestine Guinn (below) assists two ladies undergoing treatment in vapor cabinets. Other cabinets nearby offered a "dry" heat treatment, meaning they contained numerous lightbulbs for generating heat rather than using thermal water vapor.

A bath attendant in the Ozark Bathhouse helps a patron enter a stainless-steel whirlpool tub in 1960. The bathhouses in Hot Springs were constantly adding new technologies and treatments to provide their users with the latest therapies. This was done not only to contend with other facilities in town, but to compete with other spas around the country.

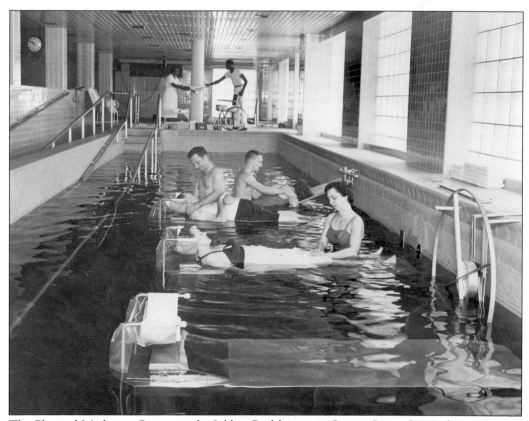

The Physical Medicine Center in the Libbey Bathhouse on Spring Street featured several large pools to accommodate multiple patients and their physical therapists simultaneously. Here, three therapists are working with their patients in a first-floor thermal pool, while attendants in the background prepare to help the patients with limited mobility out of the water.

From 1892 to 1911, trails on Hot Springs Mountain and North Mountain were developed and improved to encourage visitors to hike or ride horses for exercise on parts of the mountains not accessible by roads. The outdoor exercise regimen was encouraged as part of a holistic approach to visitor health and wellness.

Shelter houses were built on the park's mountains over the years to provide places for visitors to relax and view the valleys below. This stone shelter pavilion, built in 1924 on West Mountain, overlooks Bathhouse Row and the old Army and Navy General Hospital campus. The shelter is still in use today.

The Quapaw Bathhouse was built in 1922 and remodeled in 1929 and 1968. It closed for business in 1984. It was designed by architects Mann and Stern of Little Rock and cost $214,837 to build. Called the Platt Bathhouse during the design phase, the Quapaw stands where the Horseshoe and Magnesia Bathhouses used to be.

When the Army and Navy General Hospital complex was passed to the State of Arkansas in 1959 to be used as a vocational school, two duplexes and their garages on Reserve Avenue were retained for use by Hot Springs National Park. The former Medical Director's Residence was also conveyed to the park. Today, this duplex is used for offices by the law enforcement division.

The Roycroft Den on the third floor of the Maurice Bathhouse served a variety of purposes over the years, including, for a time, as the gymnasium. Here, two women pedal on exercise bicycles while a male bathhouse attendant adjusts the pedal tension on one cycle. When the new Maurice was remodeled in 1915, this room replaced the solarium that had been in the original building when it opened in 1912.

Architect Erskine Sunderland developed the plans for a new brick residence on Reserve Street for the park's medical director, Harry Hallock, in 1912. A Hot Springs contractor, Michael H. Jodd, won the building contract with his bid of $22,001. All through its construction, the cost of the house drew negative publicity. Dr. Hallock moved his family into the completed residence in February 1913.

The John W. Noble Fountain, named after the secretary of the interior who provided funds to help renovations in the park, was initially placed at the corner of Central Avenue and Reserve Street in 1895. In 1945, the fountain was moved to the sidewalk in front of the new Administration Building. It was a convenient resting place for pedestrians along Central Avenue.

Opening on February 1, 1912, the Buckstaff Bathhouse was a new masonry building that replaced the wooden Rammelsberg. Furnished with modern hydrotherapy equipment and a gymnasium, the new bathhouse was a popular business. Shown here is the interior of the men's waiting room, with a marble sink and tiled floors. The door at the back leads to a writing room.

Built by the park's maintenance workers in 1932, this stone cabin was initially used as a residence for the caretaker of Gulpha Gorge Campground. Visitors would sign in on the front porch of the cabin. Later, its garage was converted into a registration station for campers. The cabin has also been used as a park ranger residence, but is now reserved for the artist-in-residence program and for Volunteers-In-Parks (VIP) personnel.

Positioned between the large and expansive Eastman Hotel on the south (bottom) end and the Arlington Hotel at the upper center, Hot Springs National Park lines Central Avenue, with its jeweled bathhouses. Hot Springs Mountain on the right, West Mountain on the left, and North Mountain to the top surround the downtown area with their scenic beauty.

Park visitors enjoyed many outdoor leisure activities, such as riding in horse-drawn carriages on the roadway to the top of Hot Springs Mountain. This scenic journey presented them with stunning views of downtown, including the Arlington Hotel (right) and the new Medical Arts Building across the street.

This 1940s photograph belies the age of the Hot Springs Mountain Pagoda. Designed by architect J.G. Horn in 1911 for Lookout Point, the pagoda, with its distinctive roofline, has become an enduring icon of the park. Unfortunately, it has been plagued by vandalism since its installation. In 1914, a sign was installed listing the legal ramifications of defacing the shelter.

Above, workmen pour concrete for the construction of the Grand Promenade walkway on the hillside above Bathhouse Row. Started in 1932 as a graded dirt roadway, the route took several years to complete. Plans for the strolling path evolved over time, and in 1942 over 370 linear feet of brick paving stones were installed on a portion of it. Below, the Grand Promenade was finally completed by 1958 with the installation of plants and lighting. This picturesque walking trail presented several resting places for park patrons, some even offering tables with built-in tile chessboards. Visitors could relax and take in the natural beauty of the surrounding mountainsides above the city.

After the old Government Free Bathhouse located behind Bathhouse Row was closed, a new and final Government Free Bathhouse was constructed in 1921 on a triangle of land at the intersection of Reserve and Spring Streets. In the foreground is the Army and Navy General Hospital gate and perimeter fence.

The grand opening of the Government Free Bathhouse was celebrated on November 14, 1921, with NPS director Stephen Mather (second row, second from left); Dr. Hugh Cumming, head of US Public Health Service (second row, third from left); Dr. Hubert Work, postmaster general (first row, third from left); and Arkansas senator Joseph T. Robinson (first row, fourth from left). The other unidentified gentlemen were members of the Arkansas congressional delegation.

The new Roman Revival–style Government Free Bathhouse across Reserve Street from the Army and Navy General Hospital featured individual tubs as well as communal pools, as shown above. Led by US Public Health Service (PHS) doctors, treatment of a variety of physical ailments was available. The top floor of the two-story building housed the Government Free Bathhouse, while the lower floor contained the PHS venereal disease clinic. The Government Free Bathhouse offered the most modern equipment for therapeutic bathing, such as the stainless steel Hubbard tubs with whirlpool attachments seen below. The bathhouse offered bathing for indigent patients and African American patrons.

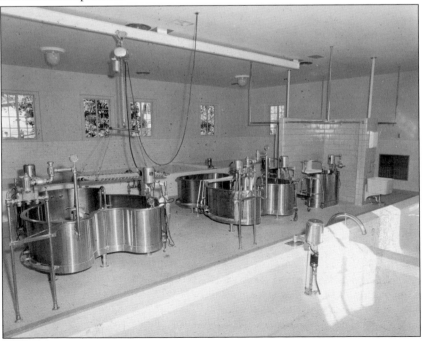

Many indigent and transient people traveled to Hot Springs to receive treatment at the Government Free Bathhouse (shown). In response to overcrowding, the Hot Springs Federal Transient Bureau was established to help people who had been displaced by the Depression. The bureau built Camp Garraday, a fenced enclosure with barracks for housing many of the male transients. Females and married couples were settled in hotels or boardinghouses.

The manicured lawns and trimmed holly hedges of Bathhouse Row in the 1940s denote the success of the bathing business. Shown here are, from near to far, the Lamar, the Buckstaff, and the twin towers of the Ozark Bathhouse. The electric light posts were installed in 1914 with five globes on each light standard.

Designed by architect Harry C. Schwebke and built by W.F. Ault, the new Superior Bathhouse was begun in 1915 (above) and completed at a cost of $68,000 (below). The building that had been erected in 1888 failed to meet the Department of Interior's rules for bathing establishments and was closed and subsequently demolished. The new 11,000-square-foot Superior Bathhouse building opened for business on February 16, 1916, and offered moderately priced baths for consumers. As the smallest bathhouse on federal property, the Superior offered only the basic hydrotherapy, mercury, and massage services. It closed its doors in November 1983.

Samuel Fordyce's bathhouse was one of the few facilities that installed a roof garden for its patrons to partake of either sunbathing or relaxing with the scenic view. A private area located on the second-floor men's side allowed nude sunbathing for men, but it was eventually phased out. The roof garden was accessed through a stairway on the third floor.

The Spanish Colonial Revival Quapaw Bathhouse was topped with a tiled dome and copper cupola. Here, workers on the scaffolding are tiling the intricate dome pattern. Built on the site of the Horseshoe and Magnesia Bathhouses, this bathhouse was designed by architects Mann and Stern, who also developed the plans for the Fordyce and Ozark.

An integral part of the national park experience has always included enjoying vistas and scenic beauty afforded at mountain overlooks. In Hot Springs, as new roads were completed and automobiles were allowed on the former carriage roads in the mountains, spaces were opened up between trees to enable visitors to stop and admire the surrounding countryside. These vehicles are at the site of the future summit overlook on West Mountain.

The "new" Hale Bathhouse with a red-brick exterior was built in 1892 and remodeled in 1914, as seen here. As with other bathhouses, the remodel was designed by Little Rock architects Mann and Stern. The redesign enlarged the structure and modified it to resemble the Classical Revival style.

The beautiful Lamar Bathhouse, with its distinctive sun porch, was designed by architects Roberts and Schwebke. The Lamar opened in 1923 and was remodeled in 1931 and again in 1946. Inside, bathers were able to choose from a variety of tub lengths to fit their height, and they could work out in the coed gymnasium.

The lobby of the Lamar is the largest of all eight bathhouses and was used as a lounge for patrons waiting for their therapeutic baths or relaxing after their therapy. In this 1950s photograph, some visitors opt to watch television during their wait. The windows were heavily draped, and awnings were placed over the windows to keep the lobby cool on summer afternoons.

Shelby Bailey, Miss Tennessee of 1956, is drinking thermal water from the Crystal Fountain in front of the Maurice Bathhouse. The unique fountain was installed in 1936, but it was later removed. Composed of tufa rock and concrete with embedded quartz crystals, the unusual drinking fountain was a standard gathering spot for photographs.

After the Arlington Hotel relocated across the street, the empty lawn space it left behind became the setting for many special events such as the May Day celebration pictured here. Music, dances, and political speeches were often held on Arlington Lawn. During World War II, the area was used for the presentation of military band concerts and medal ceremonies.

Renovations in 1941 at the Ozark Bathhouse changed the overall look of the original 1927 structure by adding wings to each side of the building and enclosing the front porch. At this stage of construction, the south wing has been assembled from brick, but the stucco has not yet been applied to the facade.

This photograph of the Ozark Bathhouse, taken after its exterior face-lift, displays the Spanish Colonial Revival architectural style. Installation of the plaster-cast window boxes and the Tree of Life cartouches on each side of the building added an impression of luxury to the 14,000-square-foot bathhouse. The Buckstaff Bathhouse is on the far right.

April 1932 was the centennial of Hot Springs Reservation–National Park, and the city turned out to help the park celebrate. History pageants, museum openings, costume balls, and a 30-float parade allowed the people of Hot Springs to demonstrate their pride in their national park and that the city's springs truly "bathe the world."

The Buckstaff Bathhouse, designed by Frank W. Gibb and Company in 1912, replaced the Victorian Rammelsberg Bathhouse. Its classic Doric columns reflected the popular Edwardian style of the time. For part of its life, the Buckstaff sported an electric sign on the roof to advertise its location on Bathhouse Row. The Lamar Bathhouse can be seen at the far right.

During the 1930s, the new Administration Building was completed (pictured), the Noble Fountain was moved to its second location away from the street corner, and the Imperial Bathhouse was demolished to prepare for the creation of a more formal south entrance to the Grand Promenade. These and other changes in park landscape and infrastructure were influenced by the National Park Service Landscape Division Design Office in San Francisco.

The Lamar Bathhouse lobby was decorated with European landscape murals, seen on the far wall in this photograph, to evoke the European spa experience. The murals and the ceiling stenciling in the lobby were painted by muralist J.W. Zelm in the 1920s. The Tennessee marble reception counter on the far right was the largest counter in any of the bathhouses.

In this west-facing photograph, taken from the Hot Springs Mountain Observation Tower, the highest point on the horizon is Music Mountain. Hot Springs Mountain is in the foreground, and North Mountain is to the right of the Arlington Hotel downtown. West Mountain extends away from the downtown valley to Music Mountain. All of these areas are part of Hot Springs National Park.

The tiled dome of the Quapaw Bathhouse wears a coating of light snow along the deserted Magnolia Promenade. The roof of the Fordyce is seen left of center. Snow on Bathhouse Row was a rarity, and this dusting may have been an omen of the changing times and attitudes ahead for the bathhouses.

Three

HARD TIMES

The introduction of modern medical technology initiated the precipitous decline of the bathing industry in Hot Springs. People no longer needed to travel to the springs from all over the country for thermal hydrotherapy and associated physical rehabilitation as previously prescribed by their physicians. Breakthroughs in science and medicine created new, more effective treatments that could be administered anywhere. After the zenith of 1947, the bathhouses at Hot Springs National Park began to see their visitation and finances wane.

With the increased availability of the automobile, people no longer had to travel by train. They could go wherever they wanted, and so America began to travel. The war had also exposed soldiers to amazing places and ideas from around the world. Back home, they shared their experiences with their families, who in turn wanted to experience the venues as well. Going to "take the cure" was no longer necessary when medicines were available in one's hometown. Travel could now be reserved for pleasure, the more exciting and exotic the better.

One by one, the bathhouses began to fall on hard times as business dried up. The first to close was the opulent Fordyce in 1962, and over the next 23 years the bathhouses shuttered their doors and took down their signs until only the Buckstaff Bathhouse remained open for business. The buildings sat empty, and the deterioration that had begun in the last years of operation accelerated at an alarming rate. The heat and humidity in the summer and the cold and rain in the winter silently ate away at the facades. Inside, plaster bubbled and fell from the walls, windows were broken, and time extracted a terrible price on the once-proud sentinels of health. The healing waters could not heal everything.

With business steadily declining, the Ozark Bathhouse closed at the end of October 1977. The addition of massage rooms to the front of the structure during the 1940s renovation, along with a laundry facility in 1958, could not stop the inevitable decline. The building sat empty for the next 29 years.

The large men's bath hall located in the center of the Ozark Bathhouse shows evidence of mold growth along the length of the wall, along with a water leak in the foreground. Many of the bathing stall doors are missing, and plaster from the ceiling and walls has fallen.

The marble bathing stall walls seem out of place next to the decayed condition of the walls in the Lamar Bathhouse. Extremes in temperature and humidity accelerate the accumulation of moisture and mold, which will grow on plaster surfaces. The white subway tiles on the walls above the tubs are still in good condition.

Stainless-steel whirlpool tubs still have their plumbing fixtures and motors in place at the Quapaw Bathhouse in 1987. This photograph was taken as part of the Historic American Engineering Record (HAER) of historic buildings. Note the paper drinking cups in the dispenser still hanging on the tiled wall.

Even the most elaborate of the bathhouses suffered while closed. The third-floor ladies lounge (later the beauty parlor) in the Fordyce displays extensive damage to the walls in the 1980s photograph seen above. The tile flooring, however, was still in excellent condition. Below, the assembly music room was connected to the ladies parlor through the door at the far end of the room. Its intricate stained-glass ceilings and stenciled walls still reflect the beauty of the original construction despite being heavily damaged by moisture. The large wooden cabinets against the left wall at one time contained John Fordyce's Native American and Spanish artifact collections.

On the first floor of the Fordyce Bathhouse, the men's steam cabinets and Sitz tub are in a state of disrepair, with parts missing. In 1962, when the bathhouse shut its doors, the rumor was that the building was to be torn down. The building manager instructed staff to remove items they wished to save. Years later, during restoration, former staff members donated original items back to the project.

Next door to the men's steam room, the Fordyce hydrotherapy room once offered a variety of treatments. In this 1980s photograph, the ornate hexagonal tile floor is heavily stained, and major parts are missing from the Scotch douche manifold on the right. The brass handrails along the walls are corroded, and the porcelain tubs are stained with rust.

There were no areas of the Fordyce Bathhouse that were not damaged by its long closure. The third-floor hallway on the ladies side of the building (at left) shows peeled and flaking plaster and damaged window frames. Without a working heating and cooling system, the building was at the mercy of the outside elements over the years. A steam cabinet in the ladies first-floor bath hall (below) seems to have survived better than the broken marble stall wall beside it. The window above the cabinet is missing its stained-glass panel, and the frame is decaying. On the far left, the edge of a broken stained-glass window is visible.

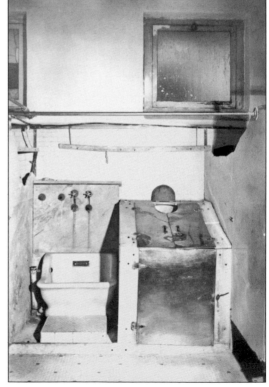

Once a hive of therapeutic activity and wellness, the gymnasium on the third floor of the Fordyce here shows the effects of years of neglect. Mold is undermining the plaster on the upper walls and the wooden ceiling. A pool of water is visible on the right side of the room near the white radiator, indicating a roof or window leak.

The last person to live in the Medical Director's Residence on Reserve Street was park superintendent Richard Maeder. He moved out of the house in 1978, and it remained empty for over 20 years. In this 1990s photograph, vines are taking over the structure, which at that time was being used for storage.

Ending its operation in 1974, the elegant Maurice Bathhouse had altered its exterior appearance very little since the renovation of 1915. In keeping with Hot Springs National Park custom, the unoccupied building is not flying the US flag on its flagpole, as shown in this 1990s photograph.

Once an inviting oasis and a technological innovation on Bathhouse Row, the therapeutic pool in the basement of the Maurice fell into disrepair after the closing of the building. The pool, added in 1931, was the largest thermal pool available on Bathhouse Row. The damages suffered by all the bathhouses over time would prove challenging to National Park Service conservators and restoration workers in the coming years.

Four

A New Lease on Life

Recognition of the historical significance of the bathhouses helped save them from ruin. Beginning with their listing in 1974 in the National Register of Historic Places, the National Park Service worked to obtain funding to protect the buildings from further deterioration and made plans on how to move ahead. Although plans to restore the structures would not be reminiscent of the formal gardens and other aspects of Mann and Stern's design from 1917, the renovation of the buildings would bring them back to the early 1900s, when they were at their pinnacle of architectural beauty.

Changes were not only happening with the bathhouses, but in other areas of the park as well. The Grand Promenade was always a wonderful pedestrian pathway for visitors to enjoy, and it was no surprise when it was designated a National Recreational Trail in 1982. It was also selected to be part of the National Historic Landmark District in 1987, along with Bathhouse Row and the formal entrance to the park.

Adaptive reuse of the buildings would be the key idea that would mean new opportunities for the bathhouses in the future. The park no longer looked at them as simply bathhouses; they would be open to other business ventures through leases and concessions that would protect the historical integrity of the buildings and bring services to park visitors.

In 1957, the park hosted a planning conference for the Park Service's Mission 66 improvement program. The Mission 66 program provided for a multitude of developments park-wide, including landscaping enhancements along the Grand Promenade. Here, park gardeners and foresters plant new trees just behind the Quapaw Bathhouse near the site of the old Government Free Bathhouse.

The 300-seat amphitheater at Gulpha Gorge Campground was part of the Mission 66 improvements to the park. It was completed in November 1965, along with a new entrance road for the campground. The new amphitheater had a rear-projection screen and a sound system for multimedia shows and ranger-led programs.

Collecting Main dump (by pass)
value at visitor center

87-3A-13

An engineering inspection of the Hot Springs Creek arch beneath the lawns of Bathhouse Row was completed in 1987. In this view, the thermal water-collecting pipe is visible, suspended from the wall of the arch. Originally, this iron pipe was insulated with redwood boards held together with tar to sustain the heat from the thermal waters as they were piped to holding reservoirs.

Park maintenance technician Mel Hayes was one of many restoration specialists called on to help bring the bathhouses back to life. Here, he is replacing the glass in a window sash for reinstallation. The preservation team removed lead paint, asbestos, and other harmful substances in preparation for adaptive reuse of the buildings.

Scientific research was reemphasized in the park beginning in the 1990s. Helen Lacy (left) and Sally Burtram from the National Aeronautics and Space Administration (NASA) in Houston are gathering thermal water samples to be used in a NASA program. Their research on the hot water taken from the Display Springs behind the Fordyce and Maurice Bathhouses detected a tiny microbe in the waters.

The Grand Promenade began as a Public Works Administration project in the 1930s, although there were walking trails along the hillside before the brick walkway was installed. In 1982, the brick and sand promenade was designated a National Recreation Trail. In 1984, the park worked to reconstruct the intricate paving pattern by replacing the sand substrate with cement.

Stone shelter houses along the mountain trails provide a welcome respite for hikers throughout the park. This North Mountain shelter also features a wayside exhibit on the flora and fauna of the park. A sign to the right warns would-be graffiti artists not to use the building as a canvas.

Looking northeast from an overlook on North Mountain, a park ranger describes to a group of visitors the topography of the Zig Zag Mountains. The area they are surveying is known today as the recharge zone for the thermal springs. Recent research has shown that the thermal water discharging today from the springs fell as rain here while the pyramids of Egypt were under construction more than 4,000 years ago.

A park ranger leads an interpretive hike along Gulpha Creek near the campground. School tours allow students to be introduced to the intricacies of the national parks and the world around them. Interaction between children and interpreters teaches young people the importance of being future stewards for the environment.

This is the latest version of the Observation Tower at the summit of Hot Springs Mountain. It was completed in 1983 and rises 216 feet in the air, providing a view of the park and the surrounding Ouachita Mountains. Visitors can ride a glass elevator to the top to enjoy the scenic beauty from multiple decks.

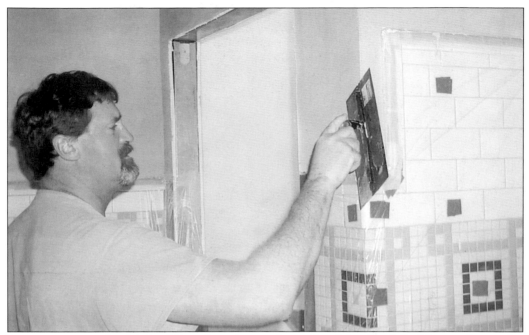

Restoration specialist Michael Powell re-plasters the walls of the Ozark Bathhouse during the building's renovation. For several years, the park employed a well-trained team of craftspeople who painstakingly removed lead paint and asbestos, replaced wiring, installed new air-conditioning systems, and repaired tile and plaster throughout each bathhouse. Slowly, the buildings were restored to life.

Restoration of the Medical Director's Residence at the intersection of Reserve and Spring Streets was completed in 2005. Today, it is home to the US Department of Agriculture Forest Service Southern Research Station, where scientists study southern pine ecology and manage upland forest ecosystems in the mid-South. (Author's collection.)

The Lamar Bathhouse is now the home of the park store, the Bathhouse Row Emporium, operated by Eastern National. The shop, which opened in 2012, sells a variety of health and wellness-related items, as well as usual national park gifts. The building also houses park staff offices and museum collection storage spaces. (Author's collection.)

Still in operation after over a century, the Buckstaff Bathhouse continues to provide the traditional-style thermal bathing experience for its patrons. The men's bathing department is located on the first floor, and the ladies' area is on the second floor. The staff also offers massage therapy as part of their bathing regimes. (Author's collection.)

Since early 2014, the Ozark Bathhouse has been the home of the park's cultural center, operated by the supporting organization Friends of Hot Springs National Park. Its galleries host special events and traveling exhibits, as well as the park's entire artist-in-residence art collection. Previously, the building was home to the Museum of Contemporary Art. (Author's collection.)

The Fordyce was restored to be the park's museum and visitor center, opening to great fanfare in 1989. It hosts more than a quarter of a million visitors per year. The museum is configured as the Fordyce was when it opened in 1915, with historic artifacts, furniture, and other museum objects on exhibit. (Author's collection.)

The only bathhouse on the row that has not been completely renovated, the empty Maurice has been re-roofed and its foundation stabilized to protect the building for the future. The restoration of its ornate lobby was begun and mostly completed, but work remains. Other areas in the facility are cleared out in anticipation of future leasing proposals. The lobby is periodically used to host special events. (Author's collection.)

Like the Buckstaff, the remodeled and updated Quapaw is today operated as a working bathhouse and spa. Instead of the traditional baths, the Quapaw provides communal bathing in four large soaking pools and a private bathing area for individuals. A café and boutique round out the amenities offered to bathers. (Author's collection.)

The Hale Bathhouse had been restored and stabilized for adaptive reuse, and over the last few years it has housed a variety of short-term leases, such as gift shops and other retail operations. Requests for proposals are periodically released by the National Park Service to allow organizations to suggest how best to use the building. (Author's collection.)

The Superior reopened in early 2013 as the Superior Bathhouse Brewery and Distillery, operated by Vapor Valley Spirits, Inc. The craft brewery uses thermal springwater to create its products and also makes its own root beer and Italian-style gelato. A full restaurant menu is offered at lunch and dinner. The business hosts special events, receptions, private meetings, and parties on the second floor. (Author's collection.)

Whittington Park is now a peaceful retreat for walkers, joggers, and visitors who want a quiet place to rest. Whittington Creek slowly meanders through the landscape within a stone-lined pathway. Summer band concerts are held in the park to commemorate the Fourth of July and other special events. (Author's collection.)

The fire ring and amphitheater at Gulpha Gorge Campground are the sites of summer campfire talks given by the interpretive rangers at the park. The lush picnic grounds and cooling waters of Gulpha Creek are still an enticing summer destination for both local and out-of-state visitors. (Author's collection.)

BIBLIOGRAPHY

Anthony, Isabel Burton, ed. *Garland County, Arkansas: Our History and Heritage.* Hot Springs, AR: Garland County Historical Society, 2009.

Berry, Trey, Pam Beasley, and Jeanne Clements, eds. *The Forgotten Expedition, 1804–1805: The Louisiana Purchase Journals of Dunbar and Hunter.* Baton Rouge: Louisiana State University Press, 2006.

Cockrell, Ron. *The Hot Springs of Arkansas—America's First National Park: Administrative History of Hot Springs National Park,* Draft. Omaha, Nebraska: US Department of the Interior, National Park Service, Midwest Region, 2013.

Farabee, Charles R. Jr. *National Park Ranger: An American Icon.* Lanham, MD: Roberts Rinehart Publishers, 2003.

Featherstonhaugh, George W., FRS, FGS. *Excursion through the Slave States, from Washington on the Potomac to the Frontier Of Mexico; with Sketches of Popular Manners and Geological Notices.* New York: Harper & Brothers, 1844.

Hill, Tom. "Biographical Sketch of Lt. Robert Stevens," *The Record.* Hot Springs, AR: Garland County Historical Society, 2013.

Hot Springs National Park. *Superintendent's Reports, 1897–2009.* Hot Springs, AR: Hot Springs National Park Archives.

Hunt, William J. Jr. *More than Meets the Eye: The Archeology of Bathhouse Row, Hot Springs National Park, Arkansas.* Lincoln, NE: National Park Service, Midwest Archeological Center, 2008.

National Park Service. *Cultural Landscapes Inventory, Gulpha Gorge Campground.* National Park Service, 2012.

———. *Cultural Landscape Report and Environmental Assessment, Hot Springs National Park.* National Park Service, January 2010.

Shankland, Robert. *Steve Mather of the National Parks.* New York: Alfred A. Knopf, 1951.